Competency Management
– The Conceptual Framework

Sudhir Warier

2014

The modern day organizational landscape is witnessing rapid changes, both in its structure and management. Managing its intangible assets is of paramount importance to an organization irrespective of its size, sector or domain, to enable it withstand the rigors of the current global economies. Only organizations that have a well defined and integrated Competency Management Framework would be able to successfully survive and compete in the knowledge economies of the future. This book introduces the basis terms, terminologies, processes associated with organizational competency management.

Competency Management
- The Conceptual Framework
by
Sudhir Warier

Table of Contents

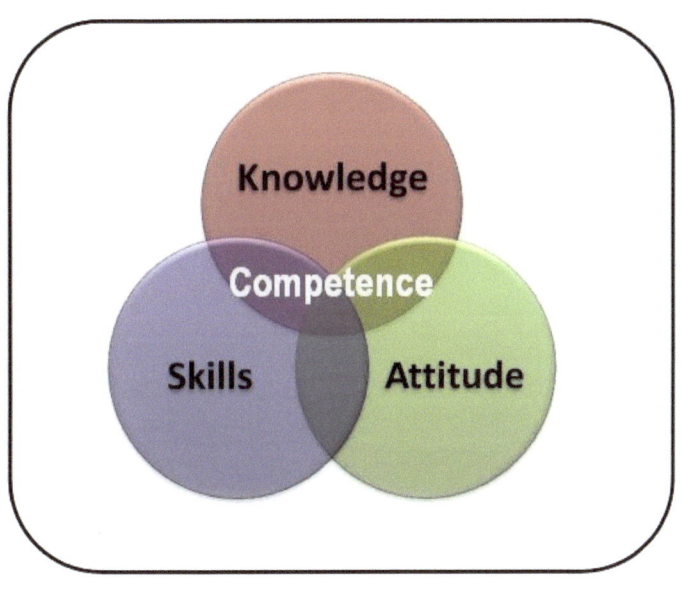

"The only true wisdom is in knowing you know nothing."

Socrates

Chapter 1

Competence - The Organizational DNA

1.0 Introduction

The origins of Competency Management can be traced to the eminent work "Arthshastra" written by Chanakya, the prime minister of the great Indian emperor Chandragupta Maurya, over 3000 years ago. Arthshastra is considered as one of the greatest work of mankind and encompasses the basics and applications of Management Sciences, Chemistry, Physics, Military and War techniques, Basic Engineering and Technologies, Ethics, Legal and Judiciary and Fiduciary system, Values, Psychology, Anthropology, Organization Behaviour and Human Resource Management.

Organizations have realized the need for developing and optimally managing their intangible resources to effectively compete in the current day recessionary economies. There is a significant amount of research being done to develop organizational mapped competencies through the deployment of Competency Mapping/Management (CM) models. Competency analysis is necessary to identify the knowledge, skills and process abilities of individuals to meet the stated organizational goals.

Competency based recruitment can shift the performance curve of employees by 10-30% resulting in increased Economic Value Added (EVA) (Hunter, Schmidt and Judiesch, 1990). Further competency based training & development (T&D) and performance management can shift the performance curve of employees positively by an average of 30-60%. It is important to note that highly productive individuals have a positive impact on the bottom line of a business enterprise.

1.1 What is Competence?

The Cambridge Advanced Learner's Dictionary defines competence as "the ability to do something well". The Collins Dictionary defines 'competence' as "Having qualifications required by the work in hand" as well as an 'ability or status' to perform the task in hand. Wikipedia defines competence as "A standardized requirement for an individual to properly perform a specific job". The second and third definitions are apt from an organizational perspective. Competencies can be defined as the cognitive, affective, behavioural and motivational personality or dispositions of an individual enabling him/her to perform well in specific situations. Thus competency can be defined as "The knowledge, skills and attributes (KSA) required by an individual to fulfill his/her organizational obligations. The development of accurate and appropriate competencies results in enhanced organizational learning, performance management while maximizing the usage of the organizational intangible assets.

Emotional intelligence (EI) is a specific set of competencies demonstrating the ability of an individual to manage their actions based on other individual's behaviours, moods, impulses and situations. Studies have shown that individuals high EI are more successful than those who are merely technically qualified.

A modern day simplified definition of Competency would be "The knowledge, skills and attributes (KSA's) required by an individual to meets his/her organizational Key Result Areas (KRA's). Competency Management encompasses all tools, techniques, methods and procedures employed by organizations to assess the available skill sets of its workforce and mapping it in accordance to its current and future requirements. CM involves an organizational need and benefits analysis, competency definition, competency assessment, model building and evaluation as well as model deployment and aims at leveraging the organizational human and Intellectual Capital (IC) to bring about a sustainable competitive advantage and tangible benefits to the organization. Human capital is the collection of intangible resources that are embedded in the members of the organization. These resources can be of three main types:

1. Competencies (including skills and know-how)
2. Attitude (motivation, leadership qualities of the top management)
3. Intellectual agility (the ability of members to adapt to changing organizational landscape)

1.2. Competency Management - Need & Benefits

In recent years a number of studies have been carried out by psychologists to understand why some people are successful in their careers while others are not. They have investigated the causes for lack of positive correlation between Intellectual Quotient (IQ) and Job performance and tried to arrive at an alternative to the traditional aptitude and intelligent testing that would predict performance. After a number of studies, David McClelland - Professor of Psychology - recognized internationally for his expertise on human motivation and entrepreneurship, arrived at such an alternate variable which he labelled as Competency. Competency can be defined as a reliably measurable, relatively enduring characteristic of an individual which is casually related to and statistically predicts effective or superior performance in a job. The following outcomes of a study by Hunter, Schmidt and Judiesch further bolstered the effectiveness of competency based Human Resources (HR) practices and made the following important conclusions (Hunter, Schmidt and Judiesch, 1990):

1. Recruitment & Selection based on competencies can shift the performance curve of employees by 10-30% resulting in increased Economic Value Added (EVA).

2. Competency-based Training & Development (T&D) and Performance Management shift the performance curve of employees positively by an average of 30- 60%.

3. The number of organizations that have adopted competency as the basis to integrate their Human Resources Systems is steadily increasing. A recent study suggests that more than 60% of the Fortune 500 companies have their HR practices based on competency.

4. Explosive growth of the information and communications technology.

5. Increased innovation and reduced cycle times.

6. Deployment of organizational knowledge management systems and effective knowledge sharing techniques.

7. Increased awareness of the importance of organizational Human capital and the associated organizational tangible benefits

1.3 Competency Management - Key Drivers

The changing and highly competitive knowledge economy has made organizations realize that their financial assets represent only a small share of total corporate assets. The most important assets are now in the form of corporate knowledge. Knowledge capital can now be calculated and forms the most important contributory influence in explaining how a firm earns its profits. The success of an organization in the future knowledge age would depend upon the effectiveness with which its knowledge capital is put to use. The following are some of the important drivers for organizational competency management initiatives:

- Recent studies have established that organizations actively engaged in managing their IC outperform others organizations in the same sector
- Knowledge Management (KM) is recognized as a core competency that organizations need to develop in order to compete successfully in today's global marketplace. KM is crucial to the adaptation and survival of organizations in the face of continuous environmental changes. The activities of knowledge acquisition, storage and distribution in a KM system enable the dynamic creation and maintenance of an enterprise's intelligence. According to the study about 80 percent of companies look to KM to play a significant role in improving competitive advantage, and consider knowledge as a strategic asset in business. KM involves a thorough, systematic approach to information repository of an organization by a sequence of collaborative processes
- The new world of business imposes the need for variety and complexity of interpretations of information outputs generated by computer systems. Such variety is necessary for deciphering the multiple worldviews of the uncertain and unpredictable future. Strategies for surviving in the new world of business cannot be 'predicted' based on a 'static' picture of information residing in the company's databases or individual mindsets. Rather, such strategies will depend upon developing interpretive flexibility based upon diverse and multiple interpretations of the future

1.4 Organizational Competency Management –Key Challenges

The rapid technological advances in all spheres of our life coupled with the ever changing political and economic landscape has brought about a drastic change in the organization, functioning and management of business enterprises. The emergence of the global knowledge economies has brought about an intense competition among business enterprises forcing them to step out from their traditional confines and bring about innovative changes in their operational setup. The primary challenges faced by organizations in their quest to manage their human capital are listed below:

- Business enterprises have to be highly innovative and agile in embracing new concepts, user preferences and the highly fluid technological advances while coming out with innovative and cost effective products and services to sustain their existence.

- In responding to the changes in the business landscape, organizations have become flexible, responsive to the ever changing needs of the customer, cost conscious, environment friendly while adopting a flatter and leaner organizational structure. In the process organizations have distanced from their most prized asset – The employee. However business enterprises soon realized that in continuously volatile economic & technology environment the only way to survive and gain competitive advantages is through the continuous development of competencies of their employees. Competitive advantage depends on the ability to effectively activate and use organizational resources. This has led organizations to analyze their internal capabilities with a specific focus on employees' competencies. This necessitates calls for a futuristic, dynamic and proactive approach to competency modelling explicitly aligned with strategic business needs and oriented to its success in the long run.

- Competency Management (CM) activities are complex to understand as well as implement primarily due to the fact that competencies are confusing and needs to be viewed from the people/employee perspective. Organizations need to understand their core competency requirements on the technical as well as the personal (behavioural) front, identify the behaviours of their best performers and finally duplicate them to drive higher productivity at all levels of the organization.

- Another important aspect is that competency descriptions are not uniformly specified nor defined across at the national/international, sectoral or organizational levels. This leads to an opaque competency description market with a multitude of competency frameworks and competency benchmarks. Thus there would not be any uniformity in competency definitions among peer organizations of the member countries within the European Union (EU) or the United States of America (USA). This also implies that there are no standardized ontologies for CM. An ontology in computer science is a formalized description of a domain usually described in a description logics language where the individuals of a domain together with all the classes and their attribute and interrelations between individuals, classes and attributes are defined. This allows automated reasoning engines to be built which by utilizing the interrelations between entities can make "intelligent" choices in different situations within the domain. As a result automated tools such as skill gap analysis, training need analysis (TNA), job search and recruitment based on individual semantically specified competency descriptions cannot be developed. The major problem with defining a common ontology for competencies is that there are so many viewpoints of competencies and competency frameworks.

A comprehensive research undertaken by Bersin & Associates covering over 700 global corporations have identified the following eight challenges in organizational talent management (Bersin & Associates, 2008):
1. Workforce Planning
2. Performance Management
3. Competency Management
4. Leadership Development
5. Succession Planning
6. Learning and Development
7. Compensation
8. Talent Management Software Systems

Another survey of over 200 senior Human Resource (HR) professionals from private and public enterprises representing 5% of the total workforce in the United Kingdom (UK) have come out with the top ten challenges facing HR resource teams and validate the results of the previously listed work. They are as listed in the Table 1 below:

Table 1- Top 10 HR Challenges

S.N	PARAMETER	RESPONDENTS(%)
1	Developing high-performing teams	66
2	Succession planning	55
3	Managing talent through change	54
4	Finding/sourcing talent externally	51
5	Developing high potential	48
6	Managing performance	46
7	Engaging people	44
8	Assessing best talent to join organization	43
9	Identifying high potential	43
10	Selecting best for internal moves	42

Summary

The wide-spread globalization of markets over recent years has resulted in businesses gradually acquiring the characteristics of an industry wherein knowledge is a significant factor in the delivery of goods and services to markets. Consequently, the development and enhancement of competencies amongst employees have come to be regarded as critical for creating effective strategies and practices to enable business survive, compete and succeed globally.

Organizations have realized the need for developing and optimally managing their intangible resources to effectively compete in the current day recessionary economies. There is a significant amount of research being done to develop organizational mapped competencies through the deployment of Competency Mapping/Management (CM) models. Competency analysis is necessary to identify the knowledge, skills and process abilities of individuals to meet the stated organizational goals.

Useful Links

1. http://www.oakenterprises.com/articles/Productivity.pdf

References

1. Hunter, J.E Schmidt, Judiesch,M.K.(1990).Individual differences in output variability as a function of job complexity. Journal of Applied Psychology, 75, 28-42
2. Bersin & Associates (2008) Organizational Talent Management. Retrieved July 1, 2010, from www.bersin.com: www.bersin.com

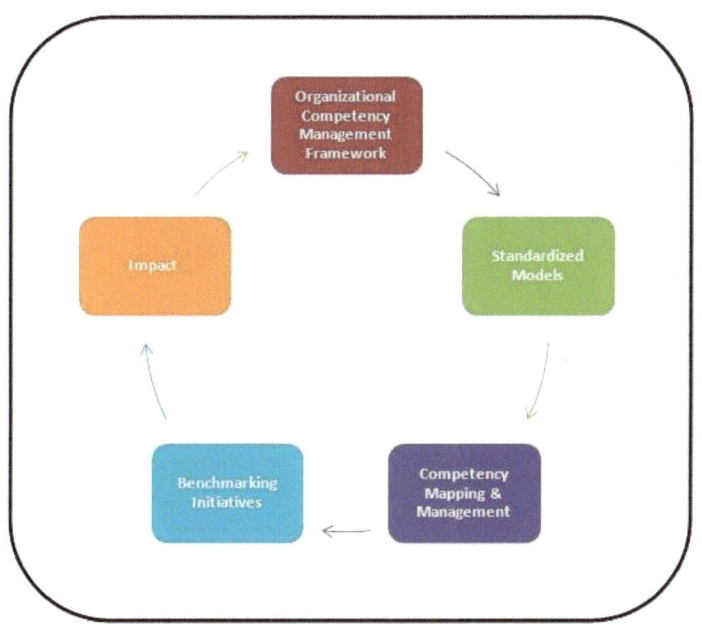

"There are no shortcuts to success, the only key is Discipline!!!"
Sudhir Warier

Chapter 2

Understanding Competencies

2.0 Classification of Competencies

Competencies can broadly be classified into two categories – Basic and Professional Competencies. Basic competencies are inherent in all individuals with only a variation in their degree of existence. For example, problem solving is a competency that exists in every individual but in varying degrees. Professional competencies in addition to the basic competencies, and are job related. For example, handling a sales call effectively is a competency that a sales personnel would be required to have. Competencies can therefore be summarized as:

Competencies = Basic Competencies + Professional Competencies

2.1 Basic Competencies

It is an established fact that each individual possesses a certain set of competencies. Only the combination and degree of these competencies differ from individual to individual. Hence, organizations have to identify the critical basic competencies required for individual employees to deliver their best in their organization. The importance of mapping the competencies proves critical for organizational success. The basic competencies encompass the following:

1. Intellectual Competencies - Those which determine the intellectual ability of a person
2. Motivational Competencies - Those which determine the level of motivation in an individual
3. Emotional Competencies - Those which determine an individual's emotional quotient
4. Social Competencies - Those that determine the level of social ability in a person

2.2 Professional Competencies

The professional competencies encompass the knowledge, experience and expertise gained by an individual employee. These include the following:

1. Motivational Competencies
   - Continual Learning
   - Perseverance
   - Achievement Orientation
2. Time Management Intellectual Competencies
   - Communication
   - Creativity
   - Analytical Ability
   - Planning and Organizing
3. Social Competencies
   - Team Work
   - Inter-personal Skills
   - Responsibility
4. Customer Satisfaction Emotional Competencies
   - Initiative
   - Optimism
   - Self Confidence
5. Leadership
   - Managing Stress
   - Managing Change

2.3 Work-Centric Competencies

From an organizational perspective competencies can be classified as:

1. Organizational Competencies — Unique factors that make an organization competitive
2. Job/Role Competencies—Things an individual must demonstrate to be effective in a job, role, function, task, or duty, an organizational level
3. Personal Competencies—Aspects of an individual that imply a level of skill, achievement, or output

Organizational competencies may further be classified as:

1. *Generic*

   These include competencies which are considered essential for all employees regardless of their function or level. Examples of generic competencies include communication skills, familiarity with office applications or productivity software

   Generic Competencies can be further sub-classified as follows:

   - *Meaning Competence*
     This helps in identifying the purpose of the existence of an organization or community and the future course of action
   - *Relation Competence*
     Creating and nurturing relations with the stakeholders of primary tasks within an organization
   - *Learning Competence*
     Exploring, exploiting and experimenting with existing processes, solutions or situations leading to efficient execution of primary organizational tasks, subsequently reflecting and internalizing the experiences
   - *Change Competence*
     Adapting in accordance with the changes in the organizational or business landscape

2. *Managerial*

   Competencies which are considered essential for employees with managerial or supervisory responsibility in any function or service. This classification is applicable to roles mapped to the middle and senior management. Managerial competencies could be more relevant for specific roles, however they are applied horizontally across the Organization, i.e. analysis and decision-making, team leadership, change management, etc.

3. *Technical/Functional*

   Specific competencies which are considered essential to perform any job in the Organization within a defined technical or functional area of work are included in this category. Examples include manufacturing, industrial process sectors, investment management, finance and administration, human resource management, etc.

The managerial competencies include the traits of systems thinking and emotional intelligence, and skills in influence and negotiation. A person possesses a competence as long as the skills, abilities, and knowledge that constitute that competence are a part of them, enabling the person to perform effective action within a certain workplace environment. Therefore, one might not lose knowledge, a skill, or an ability, but still lose a competence if the job description (what is needed to do a job well) changes.

2.4 Competency Characteristics

The characteristics list the key distinguishing features or competency attributes. The competencies have five characteristics as listed (Spencer & Spencer, 2008):

1. **Motives**

   Motives refer to things a person consistently thinks about or wants that cause action. Motives drive, direct and select behaviour towards certain actions. Example: Individuals with achievement motivation consistently set challenging goals for themselves, take responsibility for accomplishing them and use the feedback to do better

2. **Traits**

   Traits define the physical characteristics and consistent responses to situations. For example good eyesight is physical trait required of a loco or airplane pilot. Emotional Self Control and initiative are more complex consistent responses to situations

3. **Self Concept**

   Self Concept defines the attitude value or self image of an individual. Individual values are reactive or respondent motives that predict what a person would do in the short run. Example: A person who values being a leader would be more likely to exhibit leadership behaviour

4. **Knowledge**

   Knowledge relates to the information a person has in a specific work area or context. It is context specific. Example: A doctor's knowledge of the human anatomy

5. **Skill**

Skill is the ability of an individual to perform certain mental or physical tasks. Example: Mental competency includes analytical thinking. It can also be defined as the ability to establish cause and effect relationship

2.5 Competency Levels

Competency Levels are required to assess the nature and the depth of the competencies of organizational employees. This is highly helpful in mapping employees to the roles in which they are expected to deliver optimal performance. The four competency levels are as listed:

1. *Practical Competency* - An employee's demonstrated ability to perform a set of tasks

2. *Foundational Competence* - An employee's demonstrated understanding of what and why he /she are doing

3. *Reflexive Competence* - An employee's ability to integrate actions with the understanding of the action so that he / she learn from those actions and adapts to the changes as and when they are required

4. *Applied Competence* - An employee's demonstrated ability to perform a set of tasks with understanding and reflexivity

2.6 Competency Application Levels

The application levels serves as a guideline to recognize certain stages in the development of competencies. The application level provides a common frame of reference to help individuals and practitioners interpret their observations and form opinions about the development of competencies. Each level must be understood and interpreted in light of the organizational requirements. The standard levels are as listed below:

1. **Advanced**
   - Demonstrates a high level of understanding of specific competencies with the ability to independently and completely handle all related tasks
   - Frequently demonstrates application that indicates profound level of expertise
   - Can perform adviser or trainer role

- Work activities are carried out consistently with high quality standards
- Proficient
- Demonstrates a sound level of understanding of the particular competency to adequately perform related tasks, practically without guidance
- Work activities are performed effectively within quality standards
2. **Knowledgeable**
   - Demonstrates a sufficient understanding of the particular competency to be used in the work place, but requires guidance
   - Tasks or work activities are generally carried out under direction

2.7 Criterion Reference

Criterion reference is critical to the definition of competence. A characteristic is not a competency unless it predicts something meaningful in the real world. The criteria most frequently used in competence studies are (Spencer & Spencer, 2008):

1. **Superior Performance**
   This is statistically defined as one standard deviation (SD) above average performance and constitutes the level achieved by the top 1 person out of 10 in a given working situation
2. **Effective Performance**
   This usually implies a minimally acceptable level of work, the lower cut-off point below which an employee would not be considered competent to do the job

2.8 Job Roles

A Job role is a unique set of relationships, responsibilities, objectives and assigned resources. Job roles should be clearly identified, analyzed, studied and documented for identification of competencies associated with it. Job factors can be used for different applications including job design, recruitment, training need identification, remuneration scheme design, organization restructuring, competency mapping etc. The job factors include the following (Sunrise Management Consulting Services, 2008):

1. Envisioning
2. Direction

3. Organizing & Planning
4. Resource Mobilization
5. Co-ordination
6. Execution
7. Human Interaction
8. Technology
9. Creativity
10. Costs
11. Value Addition

Summary

A sound understanding of the business framework and operational scope is a prerequisite to efficiently and effectively map required competencies for specific job roles. Organizations assign responsibilities in such a way that activities requiring similar expertise and resources are entrusted to an employee or group of employees. In addition to the key business objectives an organization needs to take care of its resources, culture, employees, social obligations, statutory requirements, shareholders expectations etc. The organizations entrusts these responsibilities to its employees and provides them the requisite resources and support to execute the tasks.

Competency mapping is a strategic HR framework for monitoring the performance and development of human assets in organizations. Competency based talent management can improve both productivity and performance by identifying key characteristics of top performers and how those traits differ from average employees. These characteristics in turn can filter in a set of core competency profile that consistently leads to successful workforce.

Useful Links

1. http://www.net-temps.com/recruiters/infocus/print.htm?id=1330

2. http://www.psc-cfp.gc.ca/ppc-cpp/hrm-grh/comptcs-eng.htm

3. http://hbr.org/2001/03/understanding-competence-at-work/ar/1

4. http://en.wikipedia.org/wiki/Competence_(human_resources)

5. http://www.wikijob.co.uk/wiki/what-are-competencies

References

1. Sunrise Management Consulting Services. (2008). Model, and Method for Process Oriented Employee Performance Appraisal. Retrieved June 13, 2008, from Sunrise Consulting: http://www.sunriseconsultinggroup.net/scg/

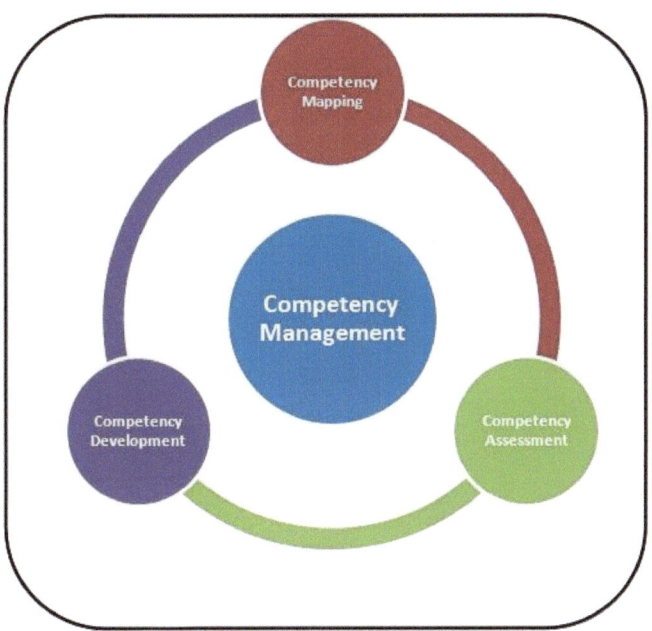

"Effective harnessing of organizational competencies is the key to lasting success"

Sudhir Warier

Chapter 3

Competency Management

3.1 Introduction

Competency management facilitates the integration of human resources planning with business planning by allowing organizations to assess the current human resource capacity based on their competencies and compare them with the capacity needed to achieve the vision, mission and business goals of the organization. This would facilitate the development of focused human capital management strategies, plans and programs to address gaps (talent acquisition, development and management).

Competency management offers organizational employees an opportunity to further personal development and adapt to the new challenges. The primary advantages include the following:

1. Increase the general employability and development of staff in changing organizations
2. Improve the quality of employees while enhancing job satisfaction
3. Strengthen the bonds and commitment among employees leading to increased organizational efficiency
4. Decreased focus on function and task orientation and thus create a more flexible attitude
5. Promote a cultural change and creating result oriented employees

Competency Management involves the developing of an Organizational Competency Framework which encompasses tailor made competency models supported by a set of competency elicitation and mapping techniques aimed at enhancing the EVA of the business enterprise.

A well designed competency management strategy facilitates the development of a optimal competency model that includes not only behaviours that are indicators of effectiveness on the job but also those required to support the organization's strategic direction, as well as develop and maintain the culture needed to achieve business results (Lusia & Lepsinger,1999) It facilitates optimal:

1. **Performance Management**

   Employee performance is evaluated against job competency requirements as well as objectives (Draganidis & Mentzas, 2006:56). In modern day performance is not only seen as "what" (objectives) an employee achieves but also viewed as "how" (competencies demonstrated) the job is carried out. Many organizations use competency-based models as a part of their employee development centres. The objective here is to assess individual' strengths and weaknesses so that future development is identified. The competency, as a measurement tool, identifies behavioural factors relevant to performance in the job. The performance management process becomes stronger when employees are appraised on both objectives (what) and behavioural performance (how), referred to as the "mixed model"

2. **Compensation Management**

   Competency based pay provides a link between competency ratings and compensation. As in the performance-management process, a mixed model approach to compensation is desirable. The important aspects of how a job is performed are ignored when organizations concentrate on pay for results only. On the other hand, organizations may not adequately evaluate results if they only focus on pay just for the use of competencies. Establishing compensation for demonstrate competencies, that is, both what is accomplished and how it is accomplished provides fairness and equity and distinguishes between superior and average performers

3. **Career Planning**

   According to McLean, the competency approach is an effective tool to be used as a criterion for career development. Competency-based career-planning systems link competencies with the development activities, which help employees learn what they need for further development (Ozcelik & Ferman, 2006: 77). They can review the needed competencies of all the positions and through comparison with the competencies they possess and identify potential positions and develop their career plans (Draganidis & Mentzas, 2006:56)

An organizational competency management system provides the following key benefits (Ashkezar & Aeen, 2012):

1. Decreased communication, training, and administration time lines
2. Managers must learn only one set of competencies and definitions for each position. It takes less training time to install each new subsystem or program because the competencies are understood, and major concepts, such as focusing on behaviour and organizing behaviour into competencies, are used throughout subsystems providing a validation mechanism
3. Information from different sources can be compared. Data from one component can be used to validate the effectiveness of the others
4. Subsystems reinforce one another
5. The use of one subsystem supports and reinforces the use of others. Using the definitions and rating scales successfully in one subsystem reminds managers the importance of using them in other activities
6. The entire system and each subsystem can be validated using a content-oriented validation strategy. This implies that the subsystem can be related to defined job requirements

3.2 Organizational Competency Management Process

A six stage organizational competency management process is outlined below. Figure 1 illustrates this model:

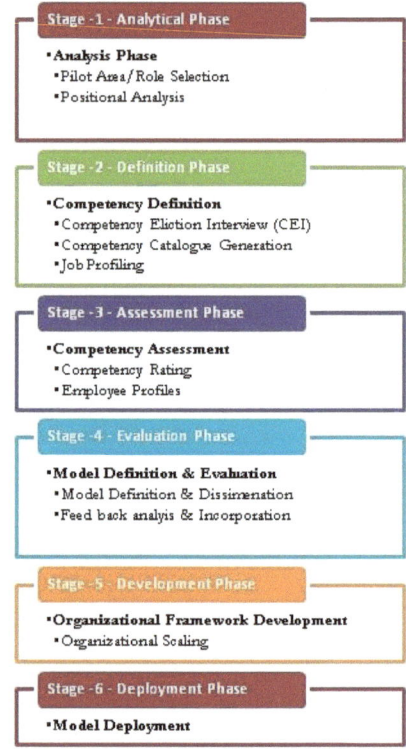

Figure 1 - Organizational Competency Management Process

STAGE – 1 ANALYSIS PHASE

A suitable pilot area within the organizational domain is selected

- Selection of positions for which competencies are to be elicited
- Positional Analysis
- Type of work
- Organizational Setting
- Organizational Structure Evaluation
- Existing competency definitions analysis (if any)

STAGE – 2 COMPETENCY DEFINITIONS

- A top-down approach is to be adopted for organizational competency modelling.
- This method employed for deriving competency requirements would be Competency Elicitation Interview.
- The initial candidates for the interview would be the front line managers.
- The results would be documented in a Job Profile, for each of the jobs analyzed.
- A Competency Catalog which documents all competency names and descriptions would be prepared.

STAGE – 3 ASSESSING COMPETENCIES

- A scale would be prepared (minimum 4 levels) to rate each competency as per the job profile.
- This would be followed by the front line managers and the employees (of the target group) rating the competencies as per the defined scale.
- The differences in rating of the manager and the employees are discussed and the feedback incorporated in the competency catalog.

STAGE – 4 COMPETENCY MANAGEMENT EVALUATION

- An implementation plan is to be drawn up
- The meeting of the entire stakeholders along with a moderator is to be arranged.
- The positive and the negative aspects of the implementation are to be noted.
- Clusters to be identified, documented and collated.

STAGES 5/6 – MODEL DEVELOPMENT & DEPLOYMENT

The next two stages consists of an organizational evaluation, followed the development and deployment of an organizational CM framework that would be integrated with KM frameworks (if any). This includes knowledge mapping activities (using software packages like Mind Mapper Rel. 2008), knowledge dissemination that includes integrating e-Learning activities to achieve competency development.

A Behavioural Anchor Rated Scale (BARS) is generally employed for the purpose of Competency Mapping. Differentiating behaviours BAR between effective and ineffective performers can be described using BAR and can subsequently be observed and anchored at points on a scale. The applicant's behaviour displayed during a behavioural interview are compared to these examples and rated accordingly. The content of the scale is developed from the job analysis and is based on responses to critical job incidents or situations. A 5 Point scale is generally employed for the purpose.

For the job profiling as well as rating the proposed Competency Mapping Model, Cohen's Cappa coefficient can be employed. Cohen's Kappa coefficient is a statistical measure of inter-ratter agreement. Cohen's Kappa coefficient is a robust measure of the agreement between two raters and takes into account the possibility of the agreement occurring by chance.

KSAO is employed for the purpose of employee profiling. KSAO refers to the job-related Knowledge, Skills, Abilities and Other characteristics that an employee must possess to successfully execute his/her organizational role. They are grouped into two major categories – technical and behavioural.

- Technical KSAOs measure acquired knowledge and technical skills.
- Behavioural KSAOs measure "soft" skills or the attitudes and approaches of an individual at work. This includes the ability to collaborate on team projects as well as the verbal communication with individuals across functional domains.

3.3 Individual Competency Management Framework

A six stage individual competency management process is outlined below. Figure 2 illustrates this model (Garrett, 2009):

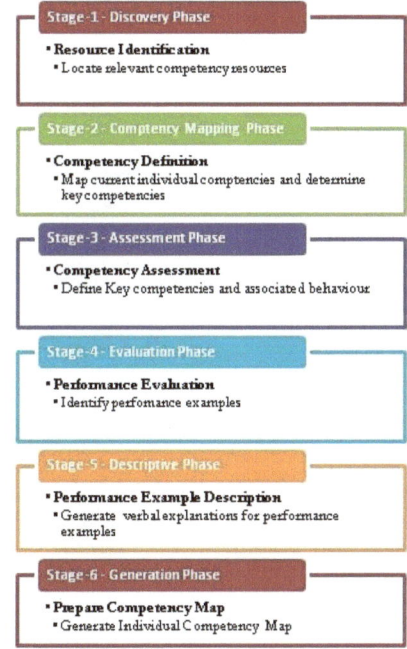

Figure 2 - Individual Competency Management Process

The following logical stages outline the individual competency mapping process:

STAGE – 1   RESOURCE IDENTIFICATION

The process commences with the identification of the competency types that an individual needs to focus on. This is followed by the search for a resource that covers the types of competencies focused by the individual. These would include online competency listings, books as well as other articles, papers, journals and allied matter (both print as well as online) on competency identification as well as individuals experienced in competency identification. This activity is supplemented with informational interviews with known experts from field of occupation as well as key organizations the individual is targeting in his/her career search.

STAGE - 2   COMPETENCY IDENTIFICATION

Individuals can identify current competencies directly by self evaluation or through the help of external consultants through interviews, standardized assessments, writing exercises, or through the use of a 360-degree feedback process that includes multi-user evaluation by individuals superiors, peers, subordinates, clients or allied groups. From this list of competencies the individual should identify the three to six key competencies that would be extremely crucial to their careers, in the present scenario. This definition is from an individual's perspective and may be highly intuitive. This is generally based on proven excellence in applying the competency or a zeal for using the competency as well as the perceived demand for the competency based on the current standing of the individual.

This list can subsequently be validated through review by experienced external consultants, ideally familiar with the individual, comparison with an established list of competencies or the usage of a 360-feedback or similar multi-rater evaluation mechanisms. Feedback from experienced mentors could also be employed for this process.

STAGE – 3   COMPETENCY ASSESSMENT

This is a time intensive activity that is performed by consultants with expertise in preparing curriculum vitae. Appropriate usage of competency development resources are solicited at this stage. It is recommended that the behaviours are worded to include specific, concrete action verbs and limit the number of behaviours per competency to six. Studies have proven that the human mind starts to lose its focus once a list exceeds seven items in length.

STAGE – 4 PERFORMANCE EVALUATION

This is one of the most critical step in an individuals endeavour for competency-based self-presentation. The individual plays an important role in this stage since he is the owner of the repository of past experiences. An individual must prepare a list of their prior work experiences, projects and other allied roles. For each item in this list the individual should note two to three concrete behavioural examples which had positive results from their effort. It should be noted that current examples have more weightages than past performances. A good practice to follow is to categorize end results and come out with examples in each of the categories.

STAGE – 5 DESCRIPTIVE ANALYSIS

It is suggested that an individual prepares a summarized list of behavioural examples organized by competency prior to an interview or performance appraisal. An individual should be clear about all the aspects of the prepared example and be ready for answering any question that may arise on them. It recommended that an individual practices the verbal delivery of the examples multiple times. This technique will ensure clarity of thought processes and help deal with any unforeseen eventualities.

STAGE – 6 GENERATE COMPETENCY MAP

For preparing a competency map the competency titles and some of the behavioural action verbs should be integrated into the descriptions of ongoing responsibilities for each position. The functional accomplishments of an individual must be well integrated with the core competencies listed. In case of freelance consultants the functional experience headings should tightly correlated with the service offerings. Further these service offerings should incorporate the consultant's core competencies. The accomplishments statements should form the nucleus of the professional experience section and the verbal statements generated in stage 5 should be condensed into accomplishment statements. The core competencies should be ideally included a separate section under the heading "Summary of Qualifications"

3.4 Challenges

The primary challenges in organizational competency management are as listed:

- Most of the CM approaches have not been feasible for organizational settings primarily due to the fact that they are not based on the psychological conceptions of human competence and performance in workplace
- Further the validity of these approaches cannot be established due to lack of mathematical formalization

- The challenge lies in the integration of psychological models into the CM methods while establishing parameters for measuring the quality of implementation. This is especially true for organizations in India
- The cultural and social diversity in India brings a unique set of challenges that needs to be addressed
- There exists a need to build flexible models that can easily be integrated into an organizational setup thereby bridging the gap between Human Resources Management (HRM) & KM practices
- The generation of an effective competency map requires careful understanding and insight into the key competencies in the individual's area of expertise and key positions of interest
- Organizational key competency listings, positional descriptions along with appropriately worded behavioural definitions are difficult to find. Thus an individual may not be able to list essential positional competencies for succeeding in an organization. To overcome this challenge an individual would have to resort to conducting informational interviews with key personnel within the organization, wherever possible. Another alternative is to rely upon one's intuition to predict key positional competencies within an organization.
- Another major challenge lies in the creation of individual competency maps. Individuals, given their limited exposure to competency mapping, may not be able to map their accomplishments into key competencies
- Further the behavioural definitions would also be inaccurate and would result in the development of "gray areas" in the prepared competency map. This challenge can, to a large extent, be overcome by hiring the services of a professional consultant with exposure to design, development and application of competencies in organizational settings. On the flip side consultants may have suitable experience in identifying knowledge and skills, but they may not be experienced in the more substantial practice of identifying organizational. This is due to the fact that a competency map in addition to knowledge also includes personal/individual competencies such as traits, thought patterns, self-esteem, judgments and other characteristics that extend beyond the technical competencies

- Further certain individuals may not be able to pen down or verbally state their past accomplishments in sufficient detail that is required to create a competency map. This could be due to a variety of factors which also includes the feeling of being pompous (in highlighting their achievements). An experience consultant should be able to overcome this problem by resorting to Competency Elicitation Interviews (CEI)

- There are numerous competencies that are not "learnable" or "developable". An experienced consultant would be able to effectively advise an individual to defocus from such competencies and locate background competencies that could be highlighted and developed.

Summary

This chapter presented the key processes involved in identifying, defining and mapping core organizational as well as individual competencies and how competencies relate to individual career development. A six layer approach to both organizational as well as individual competency development was also presented. From an organizational perspective both these processes are interlinked and cannot be isolated. Successful organizations require a synergy between organizational and individual competencies to optimally harness their intellectual and human capital. Competency management plays a critical role in achieving the organizational mission/vision through a continual cycle of development planning at both macro and micro levels. Thus this activity also includes individual planning and linkage to organizational goals.

The modern day organizational landscape is witnessing rapid changes, both in its structure and management. Managing its intangible assets is of paramount importance to an organization irrespective of its size, sector or domain, to enable it withstand the rigors of the current global economies. Only organizations that have a well defined and integrated Competency Management Framework would be able to successfully survive and compete in the knowledge economies of the future. The major organizational challenges are as listed under:

a. The deployment/application of a competency model within an organizational framework including the challenges and best practices

b. The customization of models as per organizational requirements

c. Measurement of the effectiveness of the deployed model

d. Lack of pertinent information on measuring employee competence

e. Integration of a competency model with organizational processes and support functions.

The generation of an effective competency map requires careful understanding and insight into the key competencies in the individual's area of expertise and key positions of interest. Organizational key competency listings, positional descriptions along with appropriately worded behavioural definitions are difficult to find. The next major challenge lies in the creation of individual competency maps. Individuals, given their limited exposure to competency mapping, may not be able to map their accomplishments into key competencies. Further the behavioural definitions would also be inaccurate and would result in the development of "gray areas" in the prepared competency map. This challenge can, to a large extent, be overcome by hiring the services of a professional consultant with exposure to design, development and application of competencies in organizational settings.

Useful Links

1. http://www.workitect.com/

2. http://en.wikipedia.org/wiki/Competency_management_system

References

2. Ashkezar, M. J., & Aeen, M. N. (2012). Using Competency Models to Improve HRM. Ideal Type of Management , 59- 68.

INDEX